*Barbara,
Psalms 119①!
May His Word go
and direct your
His Love For you
—Martha✗○*

THAT'S MINE!

A 14-day journey *of* declaring *and* decreeing *the* peace *of* God over *your* life

THAT'S MINE!

A 14-day journey *of* declaring *and* decreeing
the peace *of* God over *your* life

Marlena Hollis

Copyright © 2024 by Marlena Hollis.

All rights reserved. No part of this book may be used or reproduced in any form whatsoever without written permission except in the case of brief quotations in critical articles or reviews.

Printed in the United States of America.

For more information or to book an event, contact: (ptw.mhollis@gmail.com)

Book design by Marlena Hollis

Cover design by Marlena Hollis

ISBN - Paperback: 979-8-218-35285-1

About the Author

Marlena Hollis is a well-established leader in the Christian community and cosmetology industries, with over 25 years of experience as a cosmetologist, public speaker, preacher, church planter, pastor, business owner, and professional leader. Her exceptional gift for teaching and preaching the Bible has earned her a reputation as a charismatic and authoritative minister. Through the power of the Holy Spirit, she delivers prophetic revelations that inspire and enlighten her listeners, leading to powerful moments of salvation, deliverance, and prophetic revelation.

Marlena is dedicated to numerous important causes, including serving on an advisory board of an addiction recovery program. She also enjoys ministering to male and female inmates at the State Prison, spreading the message of Jesus. Marlena Hollis Ministries has partnered with the missionary group in Asia to rescue women and children from sex trafficking and slavery in Pakistan. As part of Marlena Hollis Ministries' outreach mission, the Marlena Teach Jesus program will begin airing on the NOW Television Network starting in January 2024.

Marlena and her husband, Brian, have been happily married for 27 years. They have three beautiful daughters, Abigail, Elisa, Ruthanne, and Hunter, their son-in-law. Marlena and Brian are deeply committed to their faith and have dedicated their lives to following God's lead in ministry. They believe in sharing the gospel of Jesus Christ at every opportunity and strive to live out their faith through acts of kindness and service to others. Despite the challenges that life has thrown their way, Marlena and Brian remain devoted to each other and their family. Their love for each other and their unwavering faith in God continue to be a source of inspiration to those around them.

Marlena Hollis is available for booking by emailing her personally at *ptw.mhollis@gmail.com*.

Acknowledgments

First and foremost, I would like to thank my family for their unwavering support and belief in me. My husband Brian has always been my best and most cherished supporter. My beautiful daughter, Abigail, and her husband, Hunter, are amazing young adults, and I love every moment we share. My daughters, Elisa and Ruthanne, are amazing and always willing to give me that young and sassy viewpoint that I need so that I can stay relevant and still be the cool, Jesus-loving momma to them. The love and support I receive from Brian and the girls have always been my anchor throughout this journey. I love my Hollis crew!

I am so grateful for my big, crazy, wonderful family of moms, dads, brothers, and sisters who know all my junk and still choose to let me share life and ministry with them. I love you all so much! "Mi Familia," I include you in this big, fantastic bunch! You already know my gratitude and love for you all!

Thank you to my fantastic crew of close friends for your love, support, encouragement, and belief in me. I am honestly blessed with the best!! My life is better because of you!

I want to express my heartfelt appreciation to everyone who has supported and encouraged me in launching Marlena Hollis Ministries. This book is just one of the many ways I am inspired to share my journey with all of you who have been with me on the many roads that have led me here.

Table of Contents

Introduction	11
Day 1 • Mind of Peace	13
Day 2 • Shoes of Peace	19
Day 3 • Covered by His Peace	25
Day 4 • Promise of Peace	31
Day 5 • My Defender of Peace	37
Day 6 • Peace in the Storm	43
Day 7 • Peace for my Soul	49
Day 8 • New Beginnings – Peace	55
Day 9 • Peace in my Marriage	61
Day 10 • Peace for my Children	67
Day 11 • Peaceful Sleep	73
Day 12 • Financial Peace	79
Day 13 • Unforgiveness Will Not Take My Peace!	85
Day 14 • Peace for My Past	91
Embrace Your Story For His Glory	97

INTRODUCTION

In a world filled with confusion and chaos; you can have peace. Your circumstances and life may not feel very peaceful, but you can have peace. You can have peace in the middle of your storm, in the middle of your mess, and in the middle of any tsunami that life may bring. Just as Jesus said in John 16:33, *"In this world, you will have troubles, but to be of good cheer, I have overcome the world,"* it is possible and, in fact, a priority for God to grant you peace while you live on this earth.

Before Jesus left His disciples to go to the cross, the biggest trial and sacrifice anyone has ever endured, He spoke to them about peace. Jesus gave them the gift of peace as a going-away present, you might say. This gift of peace would be what sustained them while they were instructed to wait for the arrival of the Holy Spirit. Now that must have been one powerful gift! Peace in the waiting is a whole thing!

John 14:27 (NLT) *"I am leaving you with a gift—peace of mind and heart. And the peace I give is a gift the world cannot give. So, don't be troubled or afraid."*

In this 14-day journey, I want you to start seeing peace as something other than an emotion or a state of being based on current circumstances. Instead, you must see peace as the gift that Jesus gave you! Now, if someone special to you or a prominent figure or celebrity gave you a gift, would you receive it and cherish it? Yes! You would hold so tightly to it that if someone came to steal it or even borrow it without your permission, you would be ready to fight! Well, my friend, a robber, thief, and liar are ready to steal your gift! This gift of peace should be so important that you are ready to fight if a thief even acts like he will come near. You should set up immediate boundaries and not allow access to where you hold this treasure dearly.

John 10:10 (NIV) *"The thief comes only to steal and kill and destroy; I have come that they may have life, and have it to the full."*

Starting today, begin by saying, "That's mine!" And when the enemy tries to persuade you with the best tactics, the things that have always worked, the sabotaging thoughts, and even through the voice of flesh and blood with accusations or any other devised plan against you, you must stand on the Word of God and fight! Jesus walked this earth wearing the shoes of peace daily, and He overcame the world! You and I have been given this peace and the necessary weapons to keep it! We are laying claim to what is ours, and we refuse to let go under any circumstances! Are you ready to put the Word to use in your life and to keep your peace? Let's go!

DAY 1

MIND OF PEACE

I have the mind of Christ, so, therefore, I have a peaceful mind.

When I first encountered Jesus, what caught my attention was the profound sense of peace that I felt. It was like a weight had been lifted off my shoulders, and I no longer felt burdened by the worries and anxieties that had been plaguing me. It was a feeling of calm, reassurance, and deep inner contentment that I had never experienced before. This peace drew me closer to Jesus and made me want to learn more about Him and the message of hope and love that He offers to everyone. It's amazing how something as simple as peace can have such a powerful impact on a person's life.

Before getting saved, I was overloaded with sin and shame, which caused me to live in a constant state of anxiety and depression. The mere thought of going out in crowded public places terrorized me. I never knew when a panic attack would hit me. I felt like I had no control over my life or my own emotions. My mind was filled with chaos, and I feared everything. The fear of the future, death, spiders, and people were just a few things that constantly plagued me. The list of fears seemed to grow exponentially, and it was overwhelming. I was caught in a vicious cycle of ups and downs and could not see a way off this chaotic merry-go-round! I remember when I first felt real peace at a church service. The people were so nice, and everyone seemed so happy and full of life. I was sponging on their peace, but I wanted to have this feeling forever! I wanted my peace. The only way off the merry-go-round of stress and constant drama was to J-U-M-P! It was not an easy feat, but I made the best decision of my life.

Once I accepted Jesus, I started sensing that I needed to use the Bible to help me figure out how to stay out of my previous mess and gain a new mindset. I began by reading Chapter One of 2 Timothy. I sat in bed night after night, reading verse 7 and saying it quietly to myself. Little did I know that I was using the most significant weapon God had given me to overcome the chaos in my mind. The power of God's spoken word counteracts the enemy's lies! I began to gain strength and clarity. I realize now that God's word says that I have the mind of Christ. Although I had not been taught this principle, the Holy Spirit was teaching me day by day as I leaned into the comfort of knowing Jesus.

---

1 Corinthians 2:16 (NLT) *"For who can know the LORD's thoughts? Who knows enough to teach him? But we understand these things, for we have the mind of Christ."*

2 Timothy 1:7 (KJV) *"For God hath not given us the spirit of fear; but of power, and love, and a sound mind."*

But maybe you are like me; you have been a Christian now for a long time, and this battle of the mind has set itself back up against you even after many years of walking in victory. Perhaps you have gone through some trauma and drama along your journey, and now you seem to find yourself facing the giant of fear again. Don't feel like you have failed as a Christian; rather embrace that you are human. This is the time to take back what has been stolen from you! So now is a good time to say to the thief that has come to steal your peace of mind, ***"THAT'S MINE! GIVE IT BACK!"*** You have the power and authority in Christ to set the enemy in His place through the name of Jesus, so do it! Having a little righteous anger is ok!

Declare and Decree

Today, I declare that I am taking back everything that the enemy has tried to steal from me; it has always been mine because Jesus gave it to me! The righteous decree of the Lord says that I have not been given the spirit of fear but of power, love, and a sound mindset on Christ Jesus my Lord. I have been given the power to overcome the thoughts and attacks on my mind in the name of Jesus. I have the perfect love of Christ that causes me to have supernatural strength to overcome the mean-spirited words against me. I have a sound mind because I have the mind of Christ Jesus. I declare that today, I will operate with a sound mind that is full of peace and fully guarded by the blood of Jesus. The blood of Jesus prevails against every attack on my thoughts and my peace. Peace is mine. Jesus is mine, so, therefore, victory is mine! In Jesus' name! Amen!

REFLECT

REFLECT

REFLECT

DAY 2

SHOES OF PEACE

I remember when my daughters were toddlers, and trying to put shoes on them was like shoeing a cat! Once up and running, they needed to keep their shoes on to protect those cute little feet with those chubby baby toes. We would sit down, do the "Little Piggy Went to the Market" song, put the socks on, and then, after all the fun, I would put those sweet little pumpkin shoes on. Everything was all fun and happy until *"my sock doesn't feel right!"* Suddenly, that adorable little girl became a holy terror and impossible to satisfy! Off goes the shoes, off goes the socks, and out the door goes Mom's patience! Or what about the hour spent talking them off the ledge because you tell them to put their shoes on their right feet? They insist they are right, and there is a fight to the finish to see who is stronger-willed! Is anyone besides me getting flashbacks? By the time I got to the 3rd daughter, I had learned a great way to keep my peace. It is called pick your battles. Some things are not worth being right. Can anyone hear me as I am strongly suggesting that this can be relatable to many of our relationship interactions? Peace is more valuable than having the last word or dominating the fight.

Take no offense, but many mature Christian people have not mastered the art of putting their spiritual shoes on right! We also aren't very good at learning how to keep the shoes on. Once my youngest was walking around outside without shoes on, and I told her that she could not go outside anymore with her bare feet.

She simply replied, "I don't have bear feet, I have *wittle gurl* feet!"

THAT'S MINE!

Now, that is cute, but what is not cute is when Christians refuse to put on the shoes of peace and then complain when they experience the consequences of not having this piece of armor on. You will have every opportunity to get your toes stepped on and to be offended if you do not walk with peace and insist on not going anywhere without your shoes on!

Of course, the spiritual shoes that I am talking about are the shoes of peace that Paul instructs us to wear so that we may be able to stand no matter what evil comes our way! Toddlers lose a shoe, walk around crazy with one-on and one-off- and are not fully persuaded that this is a problem. My mature and healthy friends, we must be fully persuaded that we can't go around half in and half out of peace. Battles are lost when we throw fits over petty things that may not feel comfortable or are easily offended. Being a full-grown believer is not always comfortable and cozy. So many times, we must "suck it up, buttercup" to be a peacemaker and to maintain our peace. We know the terrain is rocky, so God has given us the right piece of armor to walk this path. We are called to have our feet shod with the preparation of the gospel of peace. The right shoes are the Word of God kind of shoes.

Ephesians 6:15 (NLT) *"For shoes, put on the peace that comes from the Good News so that you will be fully prepared."*

Where do you get these shoes? In your prayer closet is where you will find the perfect-fitting shoes to wear for every occasion. If you don't get those shoes out of the prayer closet, you will be underdressed and unprepared for what you may encounter in your day. The shoes are

DAY 2

part of this gift of peace that Jesus gave you, and He had them tailor-made just for you. But even Cinderella had to speak up and take back her shoe whenever the evil stepsisters and stepmother devised a plan to steal it! It is time to speak with authority and say, "Those shoes are mine! That's my peace!" Now put them on and walk with this peace, proving He lives in you!

Philippians 4:6-7 (AMP) *"Do not be anxious or worried about anything, but in everything [every circumstance and situation] by **prayer and petition with thanksgiving**, continue to make your [specific] requests known to God. And the peace of God [that peace which reassures the heart, that peace] which transcends all understanding, [that peace which] stands guard over your hearts and your minds in Christ Jesus [is yours]."*

Philippians 4:13 (AMP) *"I can do all things [which He has called me to do] through Him who strengthens and empowers me [to fulfill His purpose—I am self-sufficient in Christ's sufficiency; I am ready for anything and equal to anything through Him who infuses me with inner strength and confident peace.]"*

Ephesians 6:15 (NLT) *"For shoes, put on the peace that comes from the Good News so that you will be fully prepared."*

Declare and Decree

I declare and decree that today is the last day the enemy will have my shoes of peace. The plan to take my authority by robbing me of peace stops NOW in the name of Jesus! All of heaven has my back, and I am more than a conqueror through Christ who strengthens me! I repent of being petty and operating in pride to be right whenever peace is the priority. I declare that I can do all things through Christ who gives me the ability, including always keeping my shoes of peace on. I am prepared in prayer and ready in the Spirit to stand, having done all to stand. I have the supernatural power to speak words of peace and bring peace into every room I go into. He goes before me and behind so I have victory in Jesus' name, Amen.

REFLECT

REFLECT

DAY 3

COVERED BY HIS PEACE

Psalms 91 is the absolute picture of being covered by the peace of God. Even as I read it aloud over myself and my family, I am filled with calm and contentment.

Psalms 91:1-16 (NIV) *"He who dwells in the shelter of the Most High will abide in the shadow of the Almighty. I will say to the Lord, 'My refuge and my fortress, my God, in whom I trust.' For he will deliver you from the snare of the fowler and from the deadly pestilence. He will cover you with his pinions, and under his wings you will find refuge; his faithfulness is a shield and buckler. You will not fear the terror of the night nor the arrow that flies by day,"*

Some days, I have no words left to say. Plain and simple, some days are hard, and some people are draining. So, instead of giving empty words from my tired soul just to check the "I prayed today" box or feeling like all I have is a list of complaints or leftovers from a long day, I go to the Word of God to fill my heart and mind with His promises.

Suddenly, I feel rejuvenated and grateful for a Father who cares more about still having the worn-out version of me in His presence than not having me at all. God always desires the real you to show up. Even if you don't feel like company, sit with God in the silence and let Him share the quiet moment with you. If you need to cry, CRY. And when you cry, don't think He will leave the room. He is the friend to the end

THAT'S MINE!

and is moved to compassion when you are just barely making it. You cannot even run Jesus off with your ugly cry! Surrender to Him all the tears and the complex emotions. He is the Master mixed media artist who can take all the junk in your mental and emotional trunk and use it to work out something beautiful and peaceful in you.

Peace looks different in different seasons and different circumstances. Sometimes, the still, small voice of the Holy Spirit whispers to your troubled soul that there are better days ahead if you stay under those magnificent wings of shelter and peace. Sometimes, there is no voice but silence. In silent times, you must rely on the truth of His word and let faith and hope be your anchor in the storm. You are going to have those days. And He is going to show up there. You don't have to deserve Him to show up. He just does. After all, the peace of Jesus is a supernatural peace that passes understanding. The Prince of Peace most certainly exceeds my understanding and expectations!

Whether you are in the hardcore throttles of grief, battling a debilitating sickness, or you are just a spouse who is tired and ready to throw in the towel, whatever your situation and whoever you are, do not, I repeat, do not waste your tears on pity and heartache, without letting Jesus into the room! Give every single tear to the **ONE** who cares for you.

Hebrews 4:15-16 (ASV) *"For we have not a high priest that cannot be touched with the feeling of our infirmities; but one that hath been in all points tempted like as we are, yet without sin."*

Psalms 56:8-10 (NLT) *"You keep track of all my sorrows. You have collected all my tears in your bottle. You have recorded each one in your book.*

DAY 3

My enemies will retreat when I call to you for help. This I know: God is on my side! I praise God for what he has promised; yes, I praise the Lord for what he has promised.

Declare and Decree

God, you know my soul is tired, and I feel less than strong, but I know that your strength is here for me. I declare that this is a temporary place and that you have a future greater than I could ever hope for or imagine planned for me. I thank You for taking every tear, and I remember Your promises to me! As I am hidden under the shadow of Your wings, I am gaining clarity of vision and strength for my future. I decree that God is faithful, and He will restore my peace, and Jesus, my Mighty Warrior, will cause the enemy to return seven times more than he has stolen from me. My God is my shield and my refuge; He is my defender and strength in every storm. I trust in Him.

In Jesus' name, Amen.

REFLECT

REFLECT

REFLECT

DAY 4

PROMISE OF PEACE

Have you ever had someone promise something to you, and they never followed through? I can understand it and get over it quickly if it happened once, but the repeat offenders are another story. I had this friend when I was a kid who would talk about all these big plans, and I would get excited, but when the day came around, she would not.

One day, I remember we planned to meet up at the park on our bikes and ride to school. I had just gotten a bike, so I was super stoked about riding with her to school. The night before, I dreamed that I was at the park waiting for my friend, and she never showed up. Well, you guessed it, that dream came true. The final straw happened on my birthday when she never even called, and when I talked to her, she said that she forgot and gave me a pretty lame gift—a coffee mug for a 9th grader. That disappointment hit hard, and after that, I decided to be her friend no longer. No one likes a friend who does not keep their promises.

One last thought about the fair weather friend: boundaries are necessary for life, my friend. With Jesus, we never have to have boundaries because He is the boundary. He is the safe place and refuge. He is a promise keeper even when we fail to be faithful or consistent. If you feel like His promises are not true for you but for everyone else, then my friend, you are missing it. If you think it is because you have messed up too much and cannot measure up to His standard, you are discounting the power of the blood that He shed which makes us righteous before our Holy God. We have been accepted into the family of God through the provision of the Cross, so we can be assured that He will come through on His promises. He will not stand you up at the park or forget your birthday. He is faithful!

Isaiah 43:1-3 (ESV) *"But now thus says the Lord, He who created you, O Jacob, He who formed you, O Israel: "Fear not, for I have redeemed you; I have called you by name, you are mine. When you pass through the waters, I will be with you; and through the rivers, they shall not overwhelm you; when you walk through fire you shall not be burned, and the flame shall not consume you. For I am the Lord your God, the Holy One of Israel, your Savior. I give Egypt as your ransom, Cush and Seba in exchange for you."*

Deuteronomy 31:6 (NIV) *"Be strong and courageous. Do not fear or be in dread of them, for it is the Lord your God who goes with you. He will not leave you or forsake you."*

2 Corinthians 1:20 (NKJV) *"For all the promises of God in Him are Yes, and in Him Amen, to the glory of God through us."*

Declare and Decree

Father, today I repent of questioning your ways whenever I do not see the details of your promises being fulfilled in my life and circumstances. Today, I declare to see through the eyes of faith and know that Jesus is my promise keeper. Today, I declare that I hope and trust in Jesus completely. Every promise that He has for me is good. I thank God that whenever I walk through the fires of life, you are with me, guiding

DAY 4

and protecting me. I declare today that when I am overwhelmed, Jesus is my peace. The flame will not consume me, and I will not dread those who come against me. You fight for me and WIN! I decree that I am a winner and I never lose because God is for me! In Jesus' name. Amen.

REFLECT

REFLECT

REFLECT

DAY 5

MY DEFENDER OF PEACE

Have you ever had someone lie about you? When you experience accusations and slander it can cause you to feel a lot of negative emotions and think some rather ugly thoughts. Did you feel crushed by all of it? It hurts to the core when friends betray you or, worse yet, a family member. Even though betrayal hurts, we must remember that it is a part of life. In those moments, we have a choice to be bitter or better. God's best for us is that we learn from it and use the experience to become stronger. I have been there more than once, and if I remain on the Lord's side, it will most likely happen again. Why would I say something so negative? Because Satan is the accuser of the believer. This is not negative talk but awareness of the imperfect flesh that we live in on this earth. We are all subject to falling short of the mark if we do not stay anchored in peace and hidden behind the cross. I believe that Jesus saves, that the Holy Spirit is alive and well in me, and that my Father God loves me unconditionally, so I do not ever have to be a victim! You and I have an enemy because Christ has an enemy, BUT that lousy liar has already been defeated!! I have peace knowing that I am never a victim, but I am always victorious because of Jesus! Look at one of my favorite scriptures in Colossians. I love it in the Passion Translation.

Colossians 2:14-15 (TPT) *"He canceled out every legal violation we had on our record and the old arrest warrant that stood to indict us."*

THAT'S MINE!

He erased it all—our sins, our stained soul—he deleted it all *and they cannot be retrieved*! Everything we once were in Adam has been placed onto his cross and nailed permanently there as a public display of cancellation. Then Jesus made a public spectacle of all the powers and principalities of darkness, **stripping away from them every weapon and all their spiritual authority and power to accuse us.** And by the power of the cross, Jesus led them around as prisoners in a procession of triumph. *He was not their prisoner; they were his!"*

Did you just read what I just read?? This is an amazing truth for believers! It says that the dark principalities that once had the authority to accuse us now have absolutely no authority, and to add to it, they have no weapons. All the enemy has is words! The saying "sticks and stones may break my bones, but words will never hurt me" is a way to defend against hurtful words spoken to you or about you. The fact is that words do hurt. My feelings get hurt but it does not make me change who I am or my position as a victorious conqueror! The truth of the Word of God always trumps the facts of your situation. Read that last sentence again. You MUST shut out the voices by speaking the TRUTH! There is a time when quiet prayers will not work for you because the voices around you are louder. Guess what you must do? **GET LOUDER!!** Start praying aloud in the Holy Spirit and let the enemy know that God's Word oversees and directs your life! Resist victim mentality by speaking over yourself the truth of who you are in Christ!

At the time, slander and accusations came out against me, I had a mad mama and some other very close family and friends who were ready with their boxing gloves to go to the accusers and set them straight! I may be a grown woman, but they were ready to be my defenders because they loved me and knew that it was an attack from the pit of

DAY 5

Hell against the call of God on my life.

My husband and I and my daughters have faced persecution as we have chosen to say Yes to the ministry. But I am here to encourage you to take your place and choose to step into the call of God on your life.

The Lord instructed me while facing that battle that He was my Defender and to have peace in the middle of the fire because I would come out with a faith-tested and sharpened sword! Because He is my Defender, I can say today that the trial made me better and not bitter. I am grateful that He defends my peace and keeps me safe, always preserving my character and refining me as I walk with Him. Who am I talking to? Has God been stirring your heart to step into action and serve in His kingdom in a bigger way? My friend, today is the day. Step in and trust that He is waiting to defend you and has already done away with that past that you are afraid of coming back to haunt you. You must stop being afraid and step up and step into what He has called you to do.

Declare and Decree

Father God, thank you for being my defender when the accusations fly. I will follow you at all costs, knowing you have already paid the highest price. I trust that as I pick up the cross, you have already walked out of the victory and are my greatest defense against anything that may come my way. I declare that you condemn every word spoken against me in judgment! Those words do not have a hold on me because You hold my past, present, and future. Knowing you are for me, I will walk in peace, and nothing can stand against me!

In Jesus' name, Amen.

REFLECT

REFLECT

REFLECT

DAY 6

PEACE IN THE STORM

A terrible tornado hit our community in the middle of writing this book. It was a normal Saturday morning; was on a Zoom call, my husband, a paramedic, was at work, and my daughters were hanging out with their spiritual sister. My call went long, and the tornado warning tones went off on my phone while I was in the middle of my conversation. We had checked the weather, and the prediction was rain with a chance of storms. The sky was clear all morning. When the second tone went off on my phone, so did the warning of the Holy Spirit inside of me!

I quickly jumped off my call and called one of my daughters to check their location and tell them to head home. The sky had suddenly turned extremely dark and ominous, and the tornado sirens in town were going off. The message came that the tornado was on the ground across town, and another one was forming. It was forming above my neighborhood. The wind had picked up, and the tail was beginning to drop down. The girls were still about 3 minutes away. I did what any Holy Ghost-filled mom would do: I stepped out on the porch, pointed at that massive dark cloud, and told it to stay away from my family! As Jesus did in Mark 4, I declared, "Peace, be still!"

You see, the peace that Jesus left for us can command the atmosphere around us and inside of us to be at peace! The wind began to shift, and the cloud moved further down past where my girls were on the road. That cloud did drop a tornado minutes later; it touched down about 3 miles north of my home, but it did not come near my dwelling. We were spared tragedy that day. I truly believe that the supernatural peace of God and knowing who I am in Christ commanded that storm to leave my territory. This peace causes you to operate in a way most will not understand. But we have to be bold! We must pray out loud with authority to maintain peace in our atmosphere! In your home, if you are experiencing a "storm," begin to pray out loud over your home. Put a demand that the atmosphere be filled with the peace of God and that all chaos must cease, in the name of Jesus!

When that storm tried to take out my family, I said, NO! Jesus said that if I speak to the mountain to be cast into the sea and believe it is done, it WILL happen. He did not say, maybe; he said it would be done, and I believe it. The weather report said that another cell was on the way with a tornado already formed, and although my girls had made it home safely, I did not stop praying. I believe this was a sneak attack from the enemy, but it was about to stop! I stepped back onto my front porch and demanded the atmosphere to be at PEACE! There was devastation across my city from the first round, but this one was not catching me off guard. Well, my friends, those reports kept coming, and I kept declaring the Word, "Peace be still, in the name of Jesus." That storm dissipated, and those clouds passed right over. You have this inside of you! It is yours to walk in! Walk in peace, speak peace, and watch how the things in your life that are out of order begin to come into order and the atmosphere shifts in your favor!

Philippians 4:7 (ESV) *"And the peace of God, which surpasses all understanding, will guard your hearts and your minds in Christ Jesus."*

Declare and Decree

DAY 6

Today, I will operate in peace and take authority over my home and spiritual atmosphere. In the middle of any storm, my God has given me the weapons I need to claim victory. When the storm shows up, I believe God has already shown up bigger. He has the ultimate authority, and Jesus has given this authority to me. I decree that when I speak to the mountain, it must obey and be cast into the sea because my God hears my prayer and will answer when I call on Him in the name of Jesus. I declare that I have the peace of God that surpasses and exceeds all human understanding; therefore, my heart is kept safe, and my mind is at peace. Because I have this supernatural peace, I am a peacemaker, willing to stand in the gap for those who need peace. From this moment forward, I will pray boldly so that the peace of God will always be established and settled in me.

In Jesus' name, Amen.

REFLECT

REFLECT

REFLECT

DAY 7

PEACE FOR MY SOUL

One of the hardest things to walk through is when everything in your world feels unsettled, and chaos seems to rule every area of your life. Life has its ups and downs, its ebb and flow. Understand that you are a nomad in a land that is not your permanent dwelling place. You are a pioneer walking out a path for someone else to follow to get to Jesus. You are only on this earth for a short period, so while you are here, we must get healing from our soul issues so that we can be about the Lord's business. We must not get stuck in the mindset, "Well, this is just my life; it will never change." I grew up in a home where there was a sense of peace, but I knew better than to get too comfortable because it gave it time, and the drama mill would start up again. Peace was temporal and superficial at best. Cycles of dysfunction created a mental paradigm that was a stronghold in my mind.

When I became a Christian, I had to cast it down and completely surrender to the Lord. Can you relate? I sincerely hope this is not your current situation, my friend. But if it is, I want to help you. You have a good Shepherd walking right beside you even in less desirable circumstances. Psalm 23 is a beautiful passage, but please don't miss the depth hidden in the text. Read it slowly with me and stop where I have added the emphasis. I want you to allow the Holy Spirit to reveal to your mind, will and emotions the care God the Father has for you.

Psalms 23 (NLT) *The LORD is my shepherd; I have all that I need.*

THAT'S MINE!

He lets me rest in green meadows; he leads me beside peaceful streams. He renews my strength. He guides me along right paths, bringing honor to his name.

Even when I walk through the darkest valley, I will not be afraid, for you are close beside me. Your rod and your staff protect and comfort me. You prepare a feast for me in the presence of my enemies. You honor me by anointing my head with oil. My cup overflows with blessings. Surely your goodness and unfailing love will pursue me all the days of my life, and I will live in the house of the LORD forever.

Can you see that this is a narrative of one's soul journey? As a pilgrim on a mission to bring glory to King Jesus, live your life in such a way that others see your walk with Jesus and want to know Him. You are not meant to stay in one place forever, but while you are in the tough places you can be at peace in your soul. But you have to believe, and you have to trust. You must see through the eyes of the Spirit beyond what your current situation looks like. Determine that you trust that the Good Shepherd is guiding you, walking with you, and preparing a place of rest for you. His unfailing love is always pursuing you! Your best days are ahead of you if you do not stop walking with the Shepherd.

Declare and Decree

The Lord is my Shepherd. He guides me and leads me through the fire and the flood. He will never leave me. Although I may be in the valley, I am not alone, and peaceful streams are up ahead. I stay so close to the Good Shepherd that I smell His sweet fragrance and abide in His

DAY 7

presence like a lamb who trusts and relies completely on the Master. I will not fear what tomorrow brings because I know that He has already prepared for me a place to rest and to be restored. My favorite place to be is in His presence. I have perfect peace in my soul because I walk with my Savior. In Jesus' name, Amen.

REFLECT

REFLECT

REFLECT

DAY 8

NEW BEGINNINGS - PEACE

The number 8, when you study the Biblical meaning of numbers, is associated with new beginnings. Although this is not a book about numbers in the Bible, I will leave that up to Troy Brewer, and I highly recommend that you look him up if this subject interests you. Please do not get in the weeds of new age religion numerology and angel numbers; this is witchcraft and not Biblical. Back to the subject, I wanted to discuss eight ways that we can be assured to keep our mind at peace. If you're reading this, I'm guessing you might be thinking about something in your life needing a new beginning, one filled with peace. Einstein is noted as saying that the definition of insanity is doing the same thing over and over again, expecting different results. By the way, it is not confirmed that Einstein said that, but it makes a valid point. Paul wrote his letters to the church in Ephesus, instructing them to be anxious about nothing. Are you anxious, nervous, worried about many things, or consumed with fear? Here is the help you need: you must do something different for a different result. The old thoughts must be replaced with new thoughts.

Philippians 4:6-8 instructs us on how to have a new, redeemed, Christlike response to handling life's challenges. Instead of being anxious, he instructed us to give thanks and pray. And then, he outlined eight new things worth thinking about. Remember that you have the mind of Christ, so your thinking must align with His.

A mind that is set on things that are true, honest, just, pure, lovely, of a good report, virtue, and praise will not have room for depression,

THAT'S MINE!

anxiety, panic, or any other negative thought that is rooted in fear. Fear cannot have a seat at your table when peace is present and seated at the head. Your peace is relying on you to make a conscious decision to think and, therefore, do something different and contrary to what the fleshly nature of man desires to do. So, if you want a different result, you must change your ways of thinking. Today, make this a day of a new beginning. Instead of worrying about your finances, give thanks for what is in your hand and watch it multiply. Whenever you hear a bad news report, speak out about God's promise, and pray with a heart assured that He is faithful. And if you are loaded with negative social media feeds or gossip columns, you most assuredly need to do something different. You will not have peace in your mind by feeding it anything other than the thoughts that are pleasing to the God of peace. Do something different today.

Isaiah 43:19 (ESV) *"Behold, I am doing a new thing; now it springs forth, do you not perceive it? I will make a way in the wilderness and rivers in the desert."*

Declare and Decree

Father God, I repent of anything known or unknown that I have allowed my mind to mediate that is not pleasing to you. I renounce all thoughts of fear and anxiety, and I thank you for being my peace. I want a new beginning in my situation, so I choose to think on new Christ-centered thoughts. Whatever things are true, whatever things are pure, whatever things are lovely, whatever things are of good report, if there is any virtue, and if there is anything praiseworthy, I

DAY 8

meditate on these things. Because I have the mind of Christ and think on these things, I am flooded with peace, and I have the blessing of the Lord flowing in my life. I am a positive influence in the lives of those around me as I speak words of positive affirmation and act in kindness towards all whom God has given me as an audience within my day-to-day life. People notice my positive outlook and are blessed to have me around.

To you be the glory, in Jesus' name, Amen.

REFLECT

REFLECT

REFLECT

DAY 9

PEACE IN MY MARRIAGE

I'm just going to say it; marriage is hard. Plain and simple, living with someone or living without someone is hard. Choose your hard. But choose according to God's plan for your life and not based upon your emotional moments that can change and will change with time and seasons. There is a principle called the 80/20 principle, simply stated in how it relates to marriage, which says that you can only get about 80% of your wants and needs from a healthy relationship, while the remaining 20% you are responsible for. I say that this is a fairly good ratio expectation. However, I encourage you to drop the expectations. You heard me right, D-R-O-P, the expectation measuring stick! First of all, that man or woman probably has no idea that you have a list set in your mind of the ideal requirements for you to be pleased with them.

Some of us have a list that only Jesus could fulfill in His glorified state of being. You are setting yourself up for misery, and your spouse is already failing almost every test when you have predetermined expectations. If you want to maintain peace of mind, focus on anything and everything your spouse is doing right. If he put the toilet seat down so you did not fall in it in the middle of the night, way to go! If she made dinner and wore that outfit that she looks so good in, tell her, and focus on it! I promise if you do this, you will see peace established in your home! Have a heart of love and grace towards your spouse, my friend, and watch God breathe His blessings on your marriage!

In the book of Ephesians, I find it fitting that Paul addresses the marriage relationship before telling them to wear the armor for spiritual battle. As a married couple, we understand that the success of our relationship depends on various factors. While some aspects may be beyond our control—I mean you can't control the behavior of your spouse—there are certain elements for which we hold responsibility. We have the power to nurture our love, trust, and respect for each other. We can choose to communicate openly and honestly, prioritize each other's needs, and work together to overcome challenges. By taking ownership of these aspects, we can create a strong foundation for our marriage and that is what Paul was telling us. First, we need to ensure that our hearts are right towards our spouses. If you are harboring offense or unforgiveness towards them, repent and allow God to soften your heart. It is our responsibility to make every attempt to love well. The influence of your right actions towards your spouse is like a ship rudder directing the path the marriage is headed in with a mighty shift of peace and wisdom coupled with love.

James 3:2 (NLT) *"Indeed, we all make many mistakes. For if we could control our tongues, we would be perfect and could also control ourselves in every other way."*

James 3:4-5 (NLT) *"And a small rudder makes a huge ship turn wherever the pilot chooses to go, even though the winds are strong. In the same way, the tongue is a small thing that makes grand speeches."*

James 3:17-18 (NLT) *"But the wisdom from above is first of all pure. It is also peace-loving, gentle at all times, and willing to yield to others. It is full of mercy and the fruit of good deeds. It shows no favoritism and is always sincere. And those who are peacemakers will plant seeds of peace and reap a harvest of righteousness."*

DAY 9

Remember, you are not battling your husband or wife, but you do have an enemy who hates your marriage. Defeat him by loving them anyway. Go back and read 1 Corinthians 13:6-8 with fresh eyes and a great attitude and heart yielded to God. Love keeps no record of wrongs. We are not measuring, keeping records, or setting expectations but we are expecting God to move mightily as we submit to Him and trust him for the outcome.

Declare and Decree

Father God, I am grateful for my spouse and the blessings of the covenant of marriage that you provide for us. I expect you to move into our home with peace and love. I choose to walk in love because love is eternal. Just as God forgives me of my sins, I forgive my spouse for any wrongdoings in our marriage. I forgive myself for dwelling on the things that are not peaceful and loving. Anything divisive against us, I declare, must be removed by the power and authority of God. No man can divide what God has put together. I declare and decree that my marriage is blessed because it is a divine covenant between God, me, and my spouse. God is our covering, and we are willing to yield to His ways and surround our hearts at the altar again.

In Jesus' name, Amen.

REFLECT

REFLECT

REFLECT

DAY 10

PEACE FOR MY CHILDREN

In Ephesians 6, Paul begins by instructing children to obey their parents in the Lord because it is the right thing to do. He reminds them that the commandment of the Lord says to honor your father and mother so that it may be well with you and you may live long on the earth. This is the first commandment that comes with a promise. But as parents, we must set our children up for success in every area of their lives, especially concerning their relationship with Father God. We make careful plans to get them on the ball team or cheerleading squad, to dance practice, or some other activity, but we must not neglect taking them to the house of God. Living life with a loving and Spirit-filled community of believers is incredibly rewarding. Not only does it bring you closer to the Father, but it is emotionally and mentally healthy for you, your spouse, and your kids. Your family needs the body of Christ, and the body of Christ needs the gifts and callings that God has gifted your family members with to add value to the church body.

But I will tell you that church hurt is real and something you may have encountered, and if you haven't, you probably will. But love covers a multitude of sins, and you and your family can grow through it if you do not let the enemy push you out. This is a great way to set your children up for a peace-filled life. It's walking with them and showing them how Jesus would handle situations both in the home and with other people that will strengthen their souls and spirits. Do not avoid letting them know how God is moving in the tough times. They need you to be transparent when you are facing challenges. Age-appropriate information will be their best teacher as they mature into Christian young men and women.

Another thing that I want to point out is that Paul made a point in verse 4 to tell fathers not to provoke their children to wrath but to bring them up in the admonition of the Lord. Simply put, this is to refrain from dictator-style parenting. Demanding without communication will create an opportunity for the enemy to sow rebellion in your child's heart. From a very young age, your child understands clear communication. As a parent, you are embarking on a lifelong journey with your child, and one of the most important factors in nurturing a healthy and fulfilling relationship with them is communication. From the very beginning, it is essential to establish a strong foundation of open and honest communication, where both you and your child feel comfortable expressing your thoughts and feelings. This means actively listening to your child, validating their emotions, and trying to understand their perspective without criticism. By doing so, you will not only build trust and strengthen your bond; you will also provide a safe and supportive environment for your child to grow and develop into a confident and secure Christian individual. Remember, communication is a two-way street, so make sure to also share your own thoughts and feelings with your child and encourage them to ask questions and express themselves freely. This does not mean that you are "best friend" style parenting; it simply means you should have a friendly relationship with your child. Don't misunderstand me; I communicate respectfully with my daughters as I expect their respect, while still being a firm parent.

It's important to remember that while the church can be a great place for children to learn about God, it's ultimately up to parents to ensure their children have a strong spiritual foundation. Raising children has its challenges but the best thing you can do for your children is to be a person of peace. Parenting from a place of peace allows you to hear from the Holy Spirit so you have divine insight and wisdom when hard situations come to your door. You want to reach a point in your spiritual journey where the Holy Spirit wakes you up in the middle of the night, guiding you on how to pray and what actions to take for your children. A mom and dad who are at peace will create a legacy for their children and the blessing of the Lord will follow your family for generations to come.

Declare and Decree

Father God, I am thankful that you are the best parent and that no one can take care of me better than you! Today, I declare the word of peace over my children. I am an influential parent filled with the power of the Holy Spirit to raise up children in the ways of the Lord so that they will not depart from Him. My home is at peace because the Prince of Peace lives within me. I am filled with wisdom and knowledge from the Holy Spirit so that I am made aware when the enemy tries to encroach on my family's territory. My children shall rise up and call me blessed because I am a (man/ woman) of God. I declare that my children will have a healthy relationship with God Almighty, their parents, and siblings. They will grow up in the admonition of the Lord, and because the Word of God is hidden in their hearts, they will not have the desire to sin against God. I decree that everything they touch will prosper and that their lives will be filled with peace and joy in the Holy Ghost.

In Jesus' name, Amen.

REFLECT

REFLECT

REFLECT

DAY 11

PEACEFUL SLEEP

Peace is a gift from God that Jesus gave to all believers. However, there are times that we go through when the circumstances are less than peaceful. I remember a time when I was experiencing a demonic attack, and it seemed like every day, a new fiery dart of the enemy was being launched against me and my family. It felt like my peace was constantly being shaken, along with my faith. Have you ever felt like a sitting duck, just minding your own business, and then, boom, out of nowhere, your world is shaken? Maybe your situation was a slow erosion that progressed so gradually that by the time the damage was done, it seemed irreparable. It can be incredibly difficult to find a sense of calm and tranquility when everything around you feels unstable or like it's on fire. The Johnny Cash song came to my mind a few times during some of my most challenging moments, "I fell into a burning ring of fire, and it burns, burns, burns…" Mine was not burning love, Mr. Cash, but the wicked schemes of the devil and his in-laws! You get my point. Here is the good news: I had a God-given fire extinguisher, and you do too! The shield of faith gives you the power to protect your heart and to extinguish EVERY fiery dart that would be sent your way. You have been given peace to put on as shoes to stand your ground and not be moved from your place of authority, especially when the accuser of the brethren begins his nasty schemes. By always wearing the armor of God, we stand strong, and with Jesus as our champion, we will win every battle. Now, that alone is reason enough to sleep in peace and wake up refreshed and ready for the next challenge!

> **Hebrews 12:2** (NIV) *"We do this by keeping our eyes on Jesus, the champion who initiates and perfects our faith. Because of the joy awaiting him, He endured the cross, disregarding its shame. Now he is seated in the place of honor beside God's throne."*

While you are in the middle of the attack, the effects of such situations can be felt in almost every area of your life. You may be doing all the things that your friends or family have suggested to get rest. You are praying, fasting, reading the Word with your cup of chamomile and lavender tea, but you are still waking up in the middle of the night with anxiety, sadness, and racing thoughts that will not quit. Regardless of the specifics, the impact of such events can be profound and long-lasting. As a result of the fiery trials I have gone through, I have learned how to use the power of peace and how to stand in faith. It may sound like I got it all together and have always been strong, but I had to walk this out to establish this level of discipline and maintain my peace. After all, it's mine! Jesus gave it to me, and neither the devil nor anyone else can have it! Say that out loud! You will make it if you do not quit!

But let me help you with some powerful scriptures that you can use to speak over yourself and anyone else who may be struggling with getting a peaceful night's sleep.

> **Proverbs 3:24** (NIV) *"When you lie down, you will not be afraid, when you lie down, your sleep will be sweet."*

John 14:27 (NIV) *"Peace I leave with you, my peace I give you. I do not give to you as the world gives. Do not let your hearts be troubled and do not be afraid."*

Matthew 11:28 (NIV) *"Come to me, all you who are weary and burdened, and I will give you rest."*

Psalm 3:5 (NLT) *"I lay down and slept, yet I woke up in safety, for the LORD was watching over me."*

Psalm 46:10 (NLT) *"Be still, and know that I am God."*

Psalm 4:8 (KJV) *"I will both lay me down in peace, and sleep: for thou, LORD, only makest me dwell in safety."*

Psalm 91:1,5,11 (NLT) *"Whoever dwells in the shelter of the Most High will rest in the shadow of the Almighty. You will not fear the terror of night, nor the arrow that flies by day. For he will command his angels concerning you to guard you in all your ways."*

Declare and Decree

From the verses above write your own declaration of peace and make it personal by putting your name in the text. Decree over your mind and heart that you have the gift of peace and that it cannot be taken from you!

REFLECT

REFLECT

REFLECT

DAY 12

FINANCIAL PEACE

There is a saying that says, "Love makes the world go around," but it seems they, whoever they are, missed it.

Money appears to be the driving force behind the world, as everything halts when the flow stops. Now, what I have just stated is not Kingdom language at all, but you may have been saying, "amen" to the previous statements because they make sense naturally.

The truth we live by is this: we live within the supernatural and divine covenant of KING JESUS; therefore, we have God as our source and provider! We do not live by a worldly mindset concerning anything, but we live by faith and operate in line with Kingdom principles governed by the Kingship of Jesus Christ, who paid for a complete redemption package that includes the salvation of our soul, health, and finances. Hallelujah!!

Let these scriptures be a source of peace for your finances.

Philippians 4:19 (NLT) *"And this same God who takes care of me will supply all your needs from his glorious riches, which have been given to us in Christ Jesus."*

Proverbs 10:22 (NLT) *"The blessing of the Lord makes a person rich, and he adds no sorrow with it."*

2 Corinthians 9:8 (NLT) *"And God will generously provide all you need. Then you will always have everything you need and plenty left over to* *share with others."*

Jeremiah 17:7-8 (NLT) *"But blessed are those who trust in the Lord and have made the Lord their hope and confidence. They are like trees planted along a riverbank, with roots that reach deep into the water. Such trees are not bothered by the heat or worried by long months of drought. Their leaves stay green, and they never stop producing fruit."*

Recently, I listened to Jim Baker, a pastor in Powell, Ohio, teach concerning Kingdom wealth. He said something so simple yet repeating it has caused me to establish peace in my household and ministry finances. He stated, "No one can take better care of me than my Father." You have probably already seen this written throughout this book because it is such a peaceful way of thinking and living. Jesus taught it in Matthew chapters 5 and 6. Jesus was all about trusting God for everything, and He made sure to talk about it all the time. He even showed us how it's done by depending on God for everything He needed while He was here on earth. Jesus wanted us to know that when we put our trust in God, we can be sure that we'll always have what we need, even if it's not what we were expecting. It's an important lesson that we can all learn from and apply to our own lives. Jesus never worried about provision or finances but was confident that His Father, our Father God would show up right on time with whatever He needed. This should bring you peace as you trust Jesus to come through for you.

Luke 12:28 (ESV) *"But if God so clothes the grass which is alive in the field today, and tomorrow is thrown into the oven, how much more will he*

DAY 12

clothe you, oh you of little faith!"

Matthew 17:27 (ESV) *"However, not to give offense to them, go to the sea and cast a hook and take the first fish that comes up, and when you open its mouth, you will find a shekel. Take that and give it to them for me and for yourself."*

I want to point out that when you are blessed, Jesus gets the glory for being the source! When Peter found the shekel, God got the glory. You must first address the negative thoughts or confessions you make concerning your finances. Repent of your lack of faith in Father God's willingness to bless you. There is breakthrough power in repentance that removes the dam of unbelief so that streams of abundant provision can begin to flow into your life. Now, decree and consistently declare the promises of provision without wavering, and watch God give you peace in your finances.

Declare and Decree

I declare that Father God takes the best care of me, and that Jesus Christ alone is my provider. I will obey when I am instructed to go get the fish and prepare in faith for the shekel! I declare that no weapon formed against my family's finances will prosper because I dwell within the protection of my father. I declare that a wall of protection has been formed around my dwelling place and the provision to maintain in perfect peace our finances. We are blessed to be a blessing, so therefore, my cup runs over for the sake of others around me. Because I seek first the Kingdom of God and His righteousness, everything I need will be added unto me. I decree that I will be blessed beyond measure and that I will give abundantly as God gives me the opportunity to sow into His people. In Jesus' name. Amen.

REFLECT

REFLECT

DAY 13

UNFORGIVENESS WILL NOT TAKE MY PEACE!

I believe that forgiveness is key to your breakthrough. When we do not forgive, our prayers are hindered, and we struggle to maintain peace and joy. When praying for people over the years for various areas of deliverance (depression, anxiety, oppression, fear, financial breakthrough, and physical healing), I have heard the Lord speak to me so many times that the person had issues of unforgiveness and that it was preventing them from receiving their miracle. He revealed to me that it was the reason that so many have been struggling for so long. Unforgiveness ultimately hinders your spiritual growth, including your ability to hear the voice of God clearly, and it robs you of your peace.

Matthew 6:14-15 (NLT) *"If you forgive those who sin against you, your heavenly Father will forgive you. But if you refuse to forgive others, your Father will not forgive your sins."*

Colossians 3:13 (NLT) *"Make allowance for each other's faults, and forgive anyone who offends you. Remember, the Lord forgave you, so you must forgive others."*

Mark 11:25 (NLT) *"But when you are praying, first forgive anyone you are holding a grudge against, so that your Father in heaven will forgive your sins, too."*

> **Luke 6:37** (NLT) *"Do not judge others, and you will not be judged. Do not condemn others, or it will all come back against you. Forgive others, and you will be forgiven."*

I have only listed a few scriptures that teach us that forgiveness is a mandatory and reasonable requirement of living for Jesus. Is it hard? Yes, but it is not an option if you want to obey the full Word of God and walk in the peace He gave to you. He forgave, and so we also have to forgive. If you wait to feel like it, you won't ever feel like it, and you will continue to aid the enemy of your soul in making you miserable, and those around you are bound to know that you are not abiding in peace. Unforgiveness contaminates the soul (mind, will, and emotions) of a person, and your words and actions become ill, sharp, and tainted with offense as they are being filtered through the bitterness. Let's ask the Lord to do a heart examination and reveal if we have hidden unforgiveness that He needs to remove from us. Jesus said that the opportunity to be offended will come. The offense sets us up for the right conditions for it to breed unforgiveness if left to fester and not dealt with immediately. So, I make it a best practice to have a regular heart check so that my peace remains established and my heart is rooted in the unconditional love of God.

Declare and Decree

Father God, I ask that you examine my heart and show me any area of my life where I may be harboring offense or unforgiveness. Holy Spirit, shine the light on the darkness and break the spell that would keep me from seeing what my flesh would try to keep hidden through

DAY 13

pride. I repent and ask for forgiveness. As the blood of Jesus is applied in this area, I declare and decree that this is no longer holding me hostage, and I also release my offender in the name of Jesus. I pray for those who have persecuted me, and I bless them and pray that Jesus would move in their hearts. I declare and decree that the power of the cross removes this blockage of unforgiveness and offense and that the blessings of peace and joy and every other promise and provision of my Father are active and overtaking me. I receive the love and kindness of my Father as the floods of blessing begin to come crashing in and refresh my soul, health, and finances. My peace is reaffirmed in Him, and I am steady in His shelter because Jesus is my strong tower and defender. Because the blood of Jesus prevails against the enemy, every malicious word curse is broken, and all demonic attacks must cease. The power of the blood of Jesus has demolished every stronghold!

In Jesus' name, Amen.

REFLECT

REFLECT

REFLECT

DAY 14

PEACE FOR MY PAST

If you are breathing, you have a past. Most of us are not proud of our past, and we are thankful that Jesus saved us from continuing the road we were traveling because it was pretty sketchy. Unless you are like my husband, Brian, who was born naturally nice and innately good, you are not trying to relive the past but would prefer never to mention it again. Even my incredibly kind-natured husband needs the blood of Jesus to be born again. But what if you have been born again, and you still are haunted by your past? I have some outstanding news! Let's read:

Psalms 139:5 (NKJV) *"You have hedged me behind and before, and laid Your hand upon me."*

The **Passion Translation** says it this way, *"You've gone into my future to prepare the way, and in kindness, you follow behind me to spare me from the harm of my past."* I love how this translation tells us that God rescues me from the harm of our past!!

I need to stop right there to take a praise break!!! Jesus, from the foundations of the world, was sent to save me from carrying the weight of my sin and shame! Jesus has followed behind me, past tense, to spare me from the harmful effects of my past. And here is the cherry on top: "He has gone into my future to prepare the way so that I would not blindly go into every ditch the enemy set for me to fall into."

THAT'S MINE!

When I first started driving, I did something, well, a lot of somethings, so dumb. I thought I had passed something in the road that looked like an animal, so I stopped in the middle of the road put my little red car in reverse, and started backing up so that I could get a better look at what was now in my rear-view mirror. My backing-up skills were not on point at this driving stage, so guess where I wound up? Yes, you guessed right. I ended up in a very deep ditch with my car now leaning over and resting on the bank. I had to get someone to come and get me out of that ditch and pray that my car was not destroyed on the right side. This could have all been avoided if I had not decided to look back at what I had passed on the road and kept moving forward. Did I also mention that I was now late for church, and so were my parents, who came to rescue me? Turns out that what I thought was an animal in the road was a pile of leaves! I learned a valuable lesson that day. The windshield is bigger than the rearview mirror because looking forward is the safest way to get to where you are going. Looking back can also cause you to get into the proverbial ditches of mind games and distorted views. You must focus forward and keep your eyes on the prize of the upward calling of Christ.

Philippians 3:13-14 (NKJV) *"Brethren, I do not count myself to have apprehended; but one thing I do, forgetting those things which are behind and reaching forward to those things which are ahead, I press toward the goal for the prize of the upward call of God in Christ Jesus."*

The Bible clearly defines what your past looks like once you are a follower of Jesus Christ. Your past is no longer empowered to have dominion over your life. But just as you read in Philippians 3:13-14, you have a part in being a partaker of the promise. You must, by an act of your own will, not your feelings, but your direct action, choose to forget and to move forward. Once you consciously decide to forgive yourself and others for the harm that was caused in your past, your feelings will have no choice but to line up. It may take a little while for the emotions to heal, but it will happen if you keep speaking and declaring the promises of God. Stop looking behind you. Stop speaking past tense. Start speaking words filled with life, light, and love. Look forward to the future of hope and promise that God our Father has planned just for you. My friend, today is the day. Step in and trust that He is waiting to defend you and has already done away with that past that you are afraid of coming back to haunt you. You must stop being afraid and step up and step into what He has called you to do.

Proverbs 24:14 (TPT) *"For then you will perceive what is true wisdom, your future will be bright, and this hope living within you will never disappoint you."*

Declare and Decree

Father God, I thank you that you have made a way through for me to forgive by washing me clean and free with the blood of Jesus. I am willing to forgive others so that the weapons of the enemy are disarmed, and all their evil schemes against me are thwarted. I will not continue to harbor unforgiveness within my mind and heart.

I forgive myself and declare that God, my father, thinks good thoughts about me continually. I forgive all transgressions and actions of those who acted as my enemy. I bless those who curse me and pray for those who took advantage of me. I also forgive myself for any part that I had in the acts of sin. I receive the full pardon of forgiveness that has been granted unto me because of the blood of Jesus Christ. I declare that forgiveness opens the doors of blessings in my life. The freedom found in Christ Jesus has given me joy and peace in abundance, and I declare that today is a day of reckoning and new beginnings as I walk forward into the high calling of Christ Jesus. My future days will be greater than my former, and I will fulfill all the assignments that God has for me to bless and further the message of Jesus on Earth. I am a carrier of peace, and everywhere I go, peace follows me. In Jesus' name, Amen.

REFLECT

REFLECT

EMBRACE YOUR STORY FOR HIS GLORY

Everyone has a journey and a unique story to tell. Sometimes, it's difficult to view our parents or elders as individuals who are still working out their stories. We tend to forget that they are ordinary humans with personal struggles, battles to face, and soul wounds that need to be healed over time. We can set unrealistic expectations. We expect them to be that strong pillar of strength and resilience we can run to at any time.

For the most part, they are strong, resilient, and full of helpful wisdom. However, when they fall short, we tend to feel disappointed and fail to empathize with them. We can quickly forget that they are human. If you want to be at peace in any relationship, let go of the expectations and ask Jesus to give you eyes to see how He sees the other person. He looked at the crowds with compassion and a yearning to heal and to set them free from sin's captive hold. He understood that they were in a process, and He yearned to be the author and finisher of their story. Even still today, Jesus gazes out over the crowd, his eyes filled with love and compassion. He sees you, and he longs for you to surrender every aspect of your life to Him. As you surrender everything to Jesus and give him the writer's pen, peace will sweep over your soul and your unique story will receive His divine kiss. If you have not fully surrendered your life to Christ or you have been in partial surrender, it is time. Let Him finish your story.

May the peace of Jesus Christ that surpasses all understanding fill your heart, mind, and soul. May it be a constant presence in your life, guiding you through every situation and circumstance. As you carry this peace with you, may it radiate from your being and touch the lives of those around you. May your words, actions, and very presence bring comfort, healing, and hope to those who need it most. May you be an instrument of peace in a world that so desperately needs it, and may you find joy and fulfillment as you grow in your faith and calling. Shalom! Shalom, that's another study for another day.

Finally

This poem by my mother, Patti Reynolds, was written from a vulnerable place and shares part of her journey to peace in her soul, as she gave Jesus the writer's quill to write her story.

<u>Seeking Peace</u>

I traveled for many aimless years—
Through heartache, trials, sorrows and tears,
When in the midst of all these cares
I realized I'd lost my Peace.
Still, I went on from day to day—
Seeking peace in my own way,
And trying to stop my mind's decay,
Still, there was no Peace.
Then came a time to realize
I was the source of my own demise,
I'd let the enemy sell me lies,
That there was no Peace.
It was then I cried out to a Savior above—
Who Reached down to me with so much Love,
A sweet spirit came and lit like a Dove,
Now I do have Peace.
For now, I choose to seek and pray
And speak only what my Lord will say,
For His words of life will rule my day,
And I will keep my Peace.

Patti Reynolds, 2023

Made in the USA
Columbia, SC
29 February 2024